Table Of Contents

01

Chapter 1: Introduction to Democratizing AI Technology

The Evolution of AI Model Development

In recent years, the field of artificial intelligence (AI) has seen a significant evolution in the development of AI models. With the increasing demand for smaller, more efficient models, researchers and developers have been exploring new techniques to optimize AI models. This subchapter will delve into the evolution of AI model development and the techniques that have made it possible to develop smaller, more efficient models.

One of the key techniques that have revolutionized AI model development is Low Rank Adaptation (LoRA). LoRA allows developers to fine-tune AI models more efficiently and cost-effectively by reducing the rank of the model's weight matrices. This technique has enabled developers to optimize AI models while maintaining high accuracy, making it a valuable tool in democratizing AI technology.

Another technique that has gained popularity in the development of smaller AI models is quantization. Quantization involves reducing the precision of the weights and activations in a neural network, resulting in a smaller model size and reduced computational complexity. By implementing quantization techniques, developers can develop smaller AI models that are more suitable for resource-constrained environments and edge computing applications.

In addition to LoRA and quantization, there are various cost-effective optimization strategies that developers can use to fine-tune AI models. These strategies not only help in reducing the computational complexity of AI models but also make it easier for developers to optimize models for specific industries and applications. By implementing these techniques, developers can democratize AI technology and make it more accessible to a wider audience.

Overall, the evolution of AI model development has been driven by the need for smaller, more efficient models that can be deployed in a variety of environments. Techniques such as Low Rank Adaptation, quantization, and cost-effective optimization strategies have played a crucial role in this evolution, making it possible for developers to fine-tune AI models more efficiently and cost-effectively. As a result, the impact of smaller, more efficient AI models on industries and applications is expected to be significant in the coming years.

The Need for Smaller, More Efficient AI Models

In the ever-evolving landscape of artificial intelligence (AI) technology, the need for smaller, more efficient models has become increasingly apparent. As AI continues to permeate various industries and applications, the demand for cost-effective and resource-efficient solutions has grown. This subchapter, titled "The Need for Smaller, More Efficient AI Models" delves into the techniques and strategies that are essential for developing compact and optimized AI models.

One of the key techniques highlighted in this subchapter is Low Rank Adaptation (LoRA), which enables developers to fine-tune AI models more efficiently. By leveraging LoRA techniques, developers can reduce the computational complexity of AI models, making them more suitable for resource-constrained environments. This not only helps in optimizing AI models for edge computing applications but also paves the way for democratizing AI technology by making it more accessible and cost-effective.

Quantization methods are another important aspect discussed in this subchapter. By employing quantization techniques, developers can develop smaller AI models without compromising on performance. This approach allows for the creation of more efficient models that consume fewer resources while maintaining high accuracy levels.

Cost-effective optimization strategies are also explored, highlighting the importance of developing AI models that are not only efficient but also economical to deploy and maintain.

The impact of smaller, more efficient AI models on various industries and applications is a key focus of this subchapter. By implementing techniques such as Low Rank Adaptation and quantization, developers can revolutionize the way AI technology is utilized across different sectors. From healthcare to finance to autonomous vehicles, the benefits of smaller AI models are far-reaching, enabling faster processing speeds, reduced energy consumption, and improved scalability.

Overall, this subchapter serves as a comprehensive guide for individuals who are interested in developing and optimizing smaller, more efficient AI models. By exploring techniques such as Low Rank Adaptation and quantization, readers can gain valuable insights into the world of AI model development and learn how to leverage cost-effective strategies to democratize AI technology. Whether you are a seasoned AI professional or a newcomer to the field, this subchapter offers valuable knowledge and practical advice for creating cutting-edge AI solutions that are compact, efficient, and impactful.

Overview of Low Rank Adaptation (LoRA) Techniques

Democratizing AI: A Comprehensive Guide to Developing Smaller, More Efficient Models

In the realm of AI model development, techniques such as Low Rank Adaptation (LoRA) are playing a crucial role in optimizing models to be smaller and more efficient. LoRA techniques involve reducing the rank of weight matrices in neural networks, which can significantly decrease the computational complexity of the model. This not only helps in reducing the memory footprint of the model but also makes it more suitable for resource-constrained environments such as edge computing applications. By implementing LoRA techniques in AI model development, developers can create models that are not only cost-effective but also performant.

Quantization methods are another key aspect of developing smaller AI models. Quantization involves reducing the precision of weights and activations in the neural network, which can lead to significant reductions in model size without compromising on performance. By quantizing a model, developers can make it more efficient and suitable for deployment on devices with limited memory and processing power. This, in turn, helps in democratizing AI technology by making it more accessible to a wider range of applications and industries.

Democratizing AI: A Comprehensive Guide to Developing Smaller, More Efficient Models

Cost-effective optimization strategies are essential for the development of smaller AI models. Techniques such as LoRA and quantization allow developers to fine-tune models more efficiently, reducing the time and resources required for model optimization. By optimizing AI models for resource-constrained environments, developers can create models that are not only smaller but also more efficient in terms of both memory and computational requirements. This can have a significant impact on industries and applications that rely on AI technology, making it more accessible and cost-effective for a wider range of use cases.

The implementation of LoRA in AI model development is a powerful tool for creating efficient models that are tailored to specific requirements. By fine-tuning models using LoRA techniques, developers can optimize models for edge computing applications, where resources are limited and performance is critical. This allows for the development of AI models that are not only smaller but also more efficient in terms of energy consumption and computational complexity. By leveraging LoRA techniques, developers can create models that are well-suited for a variety of applications, from mobile devices to IoT devices to autonomous vehicles.

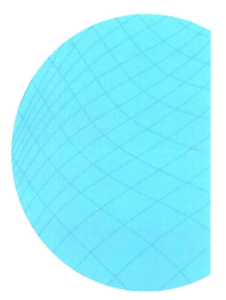

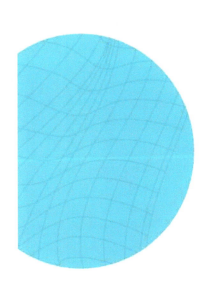

In conclusion, the development and optimization of smaller, more efficient AI models are essential for democratizing AI technology and making it more accessible to a wider range of industries and applications. Techniques such as Low Rank Adaptation (LoRA) and quantization play a crucial role in this process by reducing the computational complexity of models and optimizing them for resource-constrained environments. By implementing cost-effective optimization strategies and fine-tuning techniques, developers can create AI models that are not only smaller but also more efficient and performant. This has the potential to have a significant impact on industries and applications that rely on AI technology, making it more accessible and cost-effective for a wider range of use cases.

Introduction to Quantization Methods

In the rapidly evolving field of artificial intelligence, the development and optimization of smaller, more efficient models have become essential for democratizing AI technology. Techniques such as Low Rank Adaptation (LoRA) and quantization are making it possible to fine-tune AI models more efficiently and cost-effectively, leveling the playing field for developers and researchers alike. This subchapter will provide a comprehensive guide on the various quantization methods available for developing smaller AI models, with a focus on cost-effective optimization strategies.

Low Rank Adaptation (LoRA) is a cutting-edge technique for optimizing AI models, particularly in resource-constrained environments such as edge computing applications. By implementing LoRA in AI model development, developers can effectively reduce computational complexity while maintaining high levels of accuracy. This subchapter will delve into the intricacies of LoRA and provide practical tips for implementing this technique in AI model development.

Quantization methods offer another avenue for developing smaller AI models without sacrificing performance. By reducing the precision of numerical values within a model, quantization can significantly decrease the memory and computational requirements of AI models. This subchapter will explore the various quantization techniques available and provide insights into how developers can leverage these methods to create more efficient AI models.

Cost-effective optimization strategies are crucial for democratizing AI technology, as they enable developers to create high-performing models with limited resources. By fine-tuning smaller AI models using techniques like quantization and Low Rank Adaptation, developers can achieve impressive results without breaking the bank. This subchapter will highlight the importance of cost-effective optimization strategies and provide practical guidance on how to implement these techniques in AI model development.

In conclusion, the impact of smaller, more efficient AI models on industries and applications cannot be understated. By leveraging techniques such as quantization and Low Rank Adaptation, developers can create powerful AI models that are well-suited for resource-constrained environments and edge computing applications. This subchapter aims to equip readers with the knowledge and tools necessary to optimize AI models effectively and cost-effectively, ultimately democratizing AI technology for all.

Benefits of Cost-Effective Optimization Strategies

Democratizing AI: A Comprehensive Guide to Developing Smaller, More Efficient Models

In the world of artificial intelligence (AI), the development and optimization of smaller, more efficient models are becoming increasingly important. Techniques such as Low Rank Adaptation (LoRA) and quantization are making it possible to fine-tune AI models more efficiently and cost-effectively, which helps democratize AI technology. By utilizing these cost-effective optimization strategies, developers can create AI models that are not only smaller in size but also more efficient in their operations.

One of the key benefits of cost-effective optimization strategies is the ability to develop smaller AI models. Traditional AI models can be large and resource-intensive, making them impractical for certain applications. By implementing techniques like LoRA and quantization, developers can reduce the size of their models without sacrificing performance. This allows for the creation of AI models that are more lightweight and easier to deploy in resource-constrained environments.

Furthermore, cost-effective optimization strategies also help in democratizing AI technology. By making AI models smaller and more efficient, these techniques enable a wider range of developers to access and utilize AI technology. This can lead to more innovation and creativity in the field of AI, as developers from diverse backgrounds are able to experiment and create with these more accessible tools.

Implementing techniques like Low Rank Adaptation (LoRA) in AI model development can also have a significant impact on industries and applications. By optimizing AI models for edge computing applications, developers can improve the performance and efficiency of AI-powered devices such as smartphones, IoT devices, and autonomous vehicles. This can lead to faster and more accurate AI processing, as well as reduced energy consumption and latency.

Overall, the benefits of cost-effective optimization strategies for AI model development are clear. By utilizing techniques like LoRA and quantization, developers can create smaller, more efficient AI models that are easier to deploy, more accessible to a wider range of developers, and have a significant impact on industries and applications. Democratizing AI technology through the development of smaller, more efficient models is a crucial step towards making AI more accessible and beneficial to society as a whole.

Democratizing AI: A Comprehensive Guide to Developing Smaller, More Efficient Models

02

Chapter 2: Low Rank Adaptation (LoRA) Techniques for AI Model Optimization

Understanding Low Rank Adaptation (LoRA)

Understanding Low Rank Adaptation (LoRA) is essential for those looking to develop smaller, more efficient AI models. LoRA techniques play a crucial role in optimizing AI models, making them more cost-effective and accessible to a wider range of users. By implementing LoRA in AI model development, developers can fine-tune their models more efficiently, ultimately democratizing AI technology.

One of the key benefits of using LoRA techniques is the ability to reduce the computational complexity of AI models. This is particularly important for resource-constrained environments, where optimizing AI models for efficiency is essential. By implementing LoRA, developers can create models that are better suited for edge computing applications, allowing for real-time processing and analysis of data.

Democratizing AI: A Comprehensive Guide to Developing Smaller, More Efficient Models

In addition to reducing computational complexity, LoRA techniques also play a crucial role in developing smaller AI models. This is important for industries and applications that require models with limited storage and processing capabilities. By utilizing LoRA, developers can create models that are not only smaller in size but also more efficient in their operations.

Quantization methods are another important aspect of developing smaller AI models, and LoRA can be used in conjunction with quantization to further optimize model performance. By combining these techniques, developers can create models that are not only smaller and more efficient but also cost-effective to deploy and maintain.

Overall, understanding Low Rank Adaptation (LoRA) is essential for anyone looking to democratize AI technology through the development of smaller, more efficient models. By implementing LoRA techniques in AI model development, developers can optimize their models for resource-constrained environments, reduce computational complexity, and ultimately create models that are better suited for a wide range of industries and applications.

Implementing LoRA in AI Model Development

As the field of artificial intelligence continues to grow, there is a pressing need for more efficient and cost-effective ways to develop AI models. Techniques such as Low Rank Adaptation (LoRA) are playing a crucial role in democratizing AI technology by making it easier for developers to fine-tune their models. In this subchapter, we will explore how LoRA can be implemented in AI model development to create smaller, more efficient models that are suitable for resource-constrained environments.

Low Rank Adaptation (LoRA) techniques are becoming increasingly popular in the AI community due to their ability to optimize models in a cost-effective manner. By reducing the rank of the weight matrices in neural networks, LoRA can significantly decrease the computational complexity of AI models without sacrificing performance. This makes it an ideal tool for developers looking to create smaller models that are more suitable for edge computing applications.

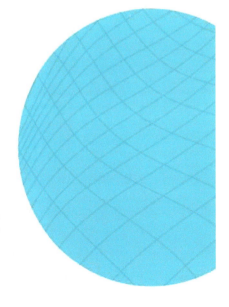

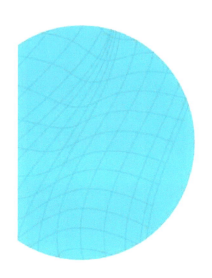

In addition to LoRA, quantization methods can also be used to develop smaller AI models. By reducing the precision of weights and activations in a neural network, quantization can further decrease the computational and memory requirements of a model. This allows developers to create more efficient models that are better suited for deployment on resource-constrained devices.

Cost-effective optimization strategies are essential for democratizing AI technology and making it accessible to a wider audience. By implementing techniques such as LoRA and quantization, developers can create smaller, more efficient models that are easier to deploy and maintain. This not only reduces the barrier to entry for AI development but also opens up new possibilities for industries and applications that were previously limited by computational constraints.

In conclusion, implementing Low Rank Adaptation (LoRA) in AI model development is a powerful way to create smaller, more efficient models that are suitable for resource-constrained environments. By combining LoRA with quantization and other optimization techniques, developers can reduce the computational complexity of their models and make AI technology more accessible to a wider audience. This has the potential to revolutionize industries and applications by enabling the deployment of AI models in new and innovative ways.

Fine-Tuning Techniques for Smaller AI Models

In the rapidly evolving field of artificial intelligence (AI), the development and optimization of smaller, more efficient models have become increasingly important. For people that want a comprehensive guide on the development and optimization of smaller, more efficient AI models, techniques such as Low Rank Adaptation (LoRA) and quantization are making it possible to fine-tune AI models more efficiently and cost-effectively. This democratization of AI technology is allowing for broader access to AI capabilities across various industries and applications.

One key technique for optimizing AI models is Low Rank Adaptation (LoRA), which focuses on reducing the computational complexity of neural networks by approximating them with low-rank matrices. By implementing LoRA in AI model development, researchers and developers can significantly reduce the size and computational requirements of their models without sacrificing performance. This technique is particularly useful for resource-constrained environments where computing power is limited.

Quantization methods are another valuable tool for developing smaller AI models. By reducing the precision of numerical values in neural networks, quantization can dramatically decrease the memory and storage requirements of AI models. This cost-effective optimization strategy is essential for edge computing applications, where computational resources are limited and efficiency is paramount.

Overall, the fine-tuning techniques discussed in this subchapter offer practical solutions for optimizing AI models in a variety of settings. By implementing Low Rank Adaptation (LoRA) and quantization methods, developers can create smaller, more efficient AI models that are well-suited for resource-constrained environments and edge computing applications. This democratization of AI technology through smaller, more efficient models has the potential to revolutionize industries and applications across the board, making AI capabilities more accessible and cost-effective for a wider range of users.

03

Chapter 3: Quantization Methods for Developing Efficient AI Models

Introduction to Quantization

Quantization is a crucial technique in the development and optimization of smaller, more efficient AI models. It involves reducing the precision of numerical values in the model, which helps to decrease the computational complexity and memory requirements. This allows for faster inference times and lower resource consumption, making it an essential tool for democratizing AI technology. In this subchapter, we will explore the fundamentals of quantization and how it can be used to fine-tune AI models more efficiently and cost-effectively.

One of the key benefits of quantization is its ability to reduce the size of AI models without sacrificing performance. By representing numerical values with fewer bits, quantization can significantly shrink the memory footprint of a model, making it easier to deploy on resource-constrained devices. This is especially important for edge computing applications, where computational resources are limited, and efficiency is paramount.

There are different methods of quantization that can be used to optimize AI models, such as post-training quantization and quantization-aware training.

Post-training quantization involves converting a pre-trained model to a quantized format, while quantization-aware training incorporates quantization during the training process to ensure that the model is optimized for lower precision values.

Both approaches have their advantages and can be used depending on the specific requirements of the AI model.

Cost-effective optimization strategies are essential for democratizing AI technology and making it more accessible to a wider audience. Techniques like quantization and Low Rank Adaptation (LoRA) play a crucial role in achieving this goal by allowing developers to fine-tune AI models efficiently and cost-effectively. By implementing these techniques, developers can create smaller, more efficient models that are better suited for deployment in a variety of industries and applications.

In the following sections, we will delve deeper into the specifics of quantization methods and how they can be implemented in AI model development. We will also explore the impact of smaller, more efficient AI models on industries and applications, highlighting the benefits of using cost-effective optimization strategies to democratize AI technology. Join us on this journey to discover the power of quantization in shaping the future of AI development.

Techniques for Reducing Computational Complexity

In the subchapter "Techniques for Reducing Computational Complexity," we will explore various methods for optimizing AI models to be smaller and more efficient. One of the key techniques we will discuss is Low Rank Adaptation (LoRA), which allows for the fine-tuning of AI models in a more cost-effective and resource-efficient manner. By implementing LoRA, developers can significantly reduce the computational complexity of their models without sacrificing performance.

Another important technique we will cover is quantization, which involves reducing the precision of numerical values in the model without compromising accuracy. Quantization is a powerful method for developing smaller AI models that are suitable for deployment in resource-constrained environments, such as edge computing applications. By optimizing the model's architecture through quantization, developers can achieve significant reductions in computational complexity while maintaining high performance levels.

Cost-effective optimization strategies will also be discussed in this subchapter, focusing on ways to streamline the development process and reduce the overall resource requirements for training and deploying AI models. By implementing efficient techniques for model development, developers can democratize AI technology by making it more accessible and affordable to a wider range of users.

The implementation of Low Rank Adaptation (LoRA) in AI model development will be explored in detail, highlighting the benefits of this technique for reducing the computational complexity of models while preserving their accuracy and performance. By fine-tuning models using LoRA, developers can achieve significant improvements in efficiency and cost-effectiveness, making AI technology more accessible to a broader audience.

Overall, the techniques discussed in this subchapter are aimed at reducing the computational complexity of AI models, making them smaller, more efficient, and easier to deploy in a variety of applications and industries. By democratizing AI technology through the development of smaller and more efficient models, we can unlock new possibilities for innovation and growth in the field of artificial intelligence.

Benefits of Quantization for AI Model Development

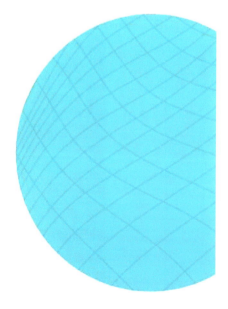

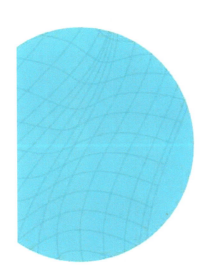

Quantization is a powerful technique that offers numerous benefits for the development of AI models. By converting the weights and activations of neural networks to a lower precision format, quantization reduces the computational complexity of the models while maintaining high accuracy levels. This results in smaller model sizes, faster inference times, and reduced memory footprint, making it an ideal solution for resource-constrained environments such as edge devices. This cost-effective optimization strategy not only saves on computational resources but also allows for the democratization of AI technology by making it more accessible to a wider audience.

One of the key advantages of quantization is its ability to fine-tune AI models more efficiently. By reducing the number of bits used to represent numerical values in the model, quantization enables faster training and deployment processes. This is particularly important for industries and applications that require real-time decision-making or have limited computational resources. With quantization, developers can achieve significant improvements in model performance without compromising on accuracy, making it a valuable tool for optimizing AI models for edge computing applications.

Low Rank Adaptation (LoRA) is another technique that is revolutionizing the development of smaller, more efficient AI models. By decomposing the weight matrices of neural networks into low-rank factors, LoRA reduces the number of parameters in the model without sacrificing accuracy. This results in faster inference times and reduced memory usage, making it a valuable tool for developing lightweight models that are suitable for deployment on resource-constrained devices. By combining quantization with LoRA, developers can further enhance the efficiency and cost-effectiveness of their AI models, paving the way for the democratization of AI technology.

Implementing quantization and LoRA techniques in AI model development requires a comprehensive understanding of the underlying principles and algorithms. Developers must carefully evaluate the trade-offs between model size, accuracy, and computational complexity to achieve optimal results. By following best practices and leveraging the latest advancements in quantization and low-rank approximation, developers can create smaller, more efficient AI models that deliver superior performance on a wide range of applications. With the democratization of AI technology through techniques such as quantization and LoRA, the possibilities for innovation and advancement in the field of artificial intelligence are endless.

04

Chapter 4: Cost-Effective Optimization Strategies for AI Models

Optimizing AI Models for Resource-Constrained Environments

In the subchapter "Optimizing AI Models for Resource-Constrained Environments," we delve into the importance of developing smaller, more efficient AI models that are tailored for environments with limited resources. This comprehensive guide is designed for individuals who are looking to optimize their AI models in a cost-effective and efficient manner. By utilizing techniques such as Low Rank Adaptation (LoRA) and quantization, developers can fine-tune their models to achieve optimal performance while minimizing computational complexity.

Low Rank Adaptation (LoRA) techniques have emerged as a powerful tool for optimizing AI models in resource-constrained environments. By exploiting the inherent low-rank structure of neural networks, LoRA allows for efficient model compression without sacrificing accuracy. This technique is particularly useful for edge computing applications where computational resources are limited, making it a valuable tool for democratizing AI technology.

Quantization methods are another essential tool for developing smaller AI models. By reducing the precision of weights and activations in neural networks, quantization can significantly decrease the memory and computational requirements of AI models. This cost-effective optimization strategy allows developers to create more efficient models that are well-suited for resource-constrained environments.

The implementation of Low Rank Adaptation (LoRA) in AI model development is crucial for achieving optimal performance in resource-constrained environments. By leveraging the benefits of LoRA, developers can fine-tune their models to meet the specific requirements of edge computing applications. This efficient AI model development process helps to democratize AI technology by making it more accessible and affordable for a wider range of industries and applications.

In conclusion, optimizing AI models for resource-constrained environments is essential for driving innovation and advancement in the field of artificial intelligence. By implementing techniques such as Low Rank Adaptation (LoRA) and quantization, developers can create smaller, more efficient models that are well-suited for edge computing applications. These cost-effective optimization strategies not only reduce computational complexity but also help to democratize AI technology by making it more accessible to a broader audience.

Efficient AI Model Development for Edge Computing Applications

Democratizing AI: A Comprehensive Guide to Developing Smaller, More Efficient Models

In the rapidly evolving field of artificial intelligence, the development and optimization of smaller, more efficient models have become crucial for a wide range of applications. For people that want a comprehensive guide on the development and optimization of smaller, more efficient AI models, techniques such as Low Rank Adaptation (LoRA) and quantization are making it possible to fine-tune AI models more efficiently and cost-effectively, which helps democratize AI technology. This subchapter will delve into the intricacies of these techniques and how they can be applied to optimize AI models for edge computing applications.

Low Rank Adaptation (LoRA) techniques have emerged as a powerful tool for optimizing AI models, particularly in resource-constrained environments. By reducing the rank of weight matrices in neural networks, LoRA can significantly decrease the computational complexity of AI models without compromising performance.

Implementing LoRA in AI model development requires a deep understanding of linear algebra and optimization techniques, but the benefits in terms of efficiency and cost-effectiveness are well worth the effort.

Quantization methods offer another avenue for developing smaller AI models that are better suited for edge computing applications. By reducing the precision of weights and activations in neural networks, quantization can drastically reduce the memory and computational requirements of AI models.

Cost-effective optimization strategies for AI model development, such as quantization, can make AI technology more accessible to a wider range of industries and applications.

By democratizing AI technology through the development of smaller, more efficient models, we can unlock new possibilities for innovation and growth in various industries. The impact of smaller, more efficient AI models on industries and applications is profound, enabling faster and more reliable AI solutions for edge computing scenarios. By fine-tuning techniques for smaller AI models, we can ensure that AI technology remains accessible and affordable for organizations of all sizes.

In conclusion, the efficient development of AI models for edge computing applications requires a combination of advanced techniques such as Low Rank Adaptation (LoRA) and quantization. By optimizing AI models for resource-constrained environments, we can maximize the performance and cost-effectiveness of AI technology. The techniques discussed in this subchapter offer valuable insights into how to reduce the computational complexity of AI models and make AI technology more accessible to a wider audience.

05

Chapter 5: Democratizing AI Technology with Smaller, More Efficient Models

The Impact of Smaller AI Models on Industries

The impact of smaller AI models on industries is profound and far-reaching. As technology continues to advance, the need for more efficient and cost-effective AI models has become increasingly apparent. Techniques such as Low Rank Adaptation (LoRA) and quantization are making it possible to fine-tune AI models more efficiently and cost-effectively, which is helping to democratize AI technology. This comprehensive guide delves into the various techniques and strategies for developing smaller, more efficient AI models, and explores how these advancements are revolutionizing industries across the board.

Democratizing AI: A Comprehensive Guide to Developing Smaller, More Efficient Models

One of the key techniques discussed in this subchapter is Low Rank Adaptation (LoRA), which offers a powerful method for optimizing AI models. By reducing the rank of a model's weight matrices, LoRA can significantly decrease the computational complexity of the model without sacrificing performance. This makes it an invaluable tool for developing smaller, more efficient AI models that are well-suited for resource-constrained environments and edge computing applications.

Quantization is another important technique explored in this guide, which involves reducing the precision of numerical values in a model. This process can lead to substantial reductions in model size and computational requirements, making it an essential tool for developing smaller AI models that are both cost-effective and efficient. By implementing quantization methods, developers can create models that are better suited for a wide range of applications and industries.

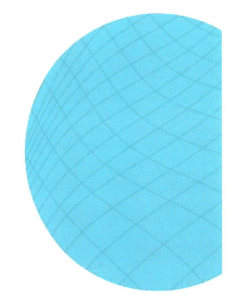

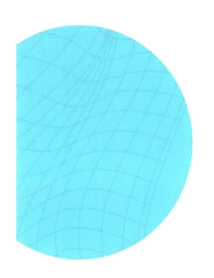

Cost-effective optimization strategies are also crucial for the development of smaller AI models. By leveraging techniques such as LoRA and quantization, developers can fine-tune their models more efficiently and affordably, which is essential for democratizing AI technology. These strategies enable organizations to implement AI solutions that were previously out of reach due to cost or resource constraints, opening up new opportunities for innovation and growth across various industries.

In conclusion, the impact of smaller, more efficient AI models on industries is undeniable. By implementing techniques like Low Rank Adaptation (LoRA) and quantization, developers can optimize their models more effectively and cost-efficiently, democratizing AI technology in the process. This comprehensive guide provides valuable insights into the development and optimization of smaller AI models, offering a roadmap for organizations looking to harness the power of AI in a more accessible and scalable way.

Applications of Small, Efficient AI Models

Democratizing AI: A Comprehensive Guide to Developing Smaller, More Efficient Models

In recent years, there has been a growing demand for smaller and more efficient AI models that can be easily deployed in a variety of applications. This shift towards developing compact models has been driven by the need to reduce computational costs, improve performance, and enable AI technology to be more accessible to a wider audience. Techniques such as Low Rank Adaptation (LoRA) and quantization are at the forefront of this movement, making it possible to fine-tune AI models more efficiently and cost-effectively. These methods are revolutionizing the field of AI by democratizing the technology and opening up new possibilities for innovation.

One of the key techniques for optimizing AI models is Low Rank Adaptation (LoRA), which focuses on reducing the computational complexity of deep learning models. By decomposing the weight matrices of neural networks into low-rank matrices, LoRA enables more efficient training and inference, leading to significant improvements in performance. This approach is particularly useful for resource-constrained environments where computational resources are limited, making it an essential tool for developing AI models that can operate efficiently on edge devices.

Quantization is another powerful method for developing smaller AI models by reducing the precision of numerical values in neural networks. By representing weights and activations with fewer bits, quantization can significantly decrease the memory and computational requirements of AI models without sacrificing accuracy. This technique is essential for optimizing models for edge computing applications, where limited storage and processing capabilities necessitate compact and efficient solutions.

Cost-effective optimization strategies are crucial for democratizing AI technology and making it more accessible to a wider range of industries and applications. By leveraging techniques like LoRA and quantization, developers can create smaller, more efficient AI models that are not only easier to deploy but also more affordable to maintain. This shift towards cost-effective optimization is reshaping the landscape of AI development, enabling organizations of all sizes to harness the power of artificial intelligence in innovative ways.

Overall, the development and optimization of smaller, more efficient AI models have far-reaching implications for industries and applications across the board. By implementing techniques such as Low Rank Adaptation (LoRA) and quantization, developers can create AI solutions that are not only more resource-efficient but also more scalable and versatile. The democratization of AI technology through smaller models is opening up new opportunities for innovation and driving the adoption of AI in a wide range of fields, from healthcare and finance to autonomous vehicles and smart home devices.

06

Chapter 6:
Conclusion

Future Trends in AI Model Development

In recent years, there has been a significant shift towards developing smaller, more efficient AI models. This trend is driven by the need for cost-effective and resource-efficient solutions that can be deployed in a wide range of applications. Techniques such as Low Rank Adaptation (LoRA) and quantization are playing a crucial role in making it possible to fine-tune AI models more efficiently and effectively. These methods not only reduce the computational complexity of AI models but also help democratize AI technology by making it more accessible to a wider audience.

Low Rank Adaptation (LoRA) is a powerful technique that allows developers to optimize AI models by reducing their rank. By decomposing the original model into low-rank components, LoRA can significantly reduce the computational overhead while maintaining high levels of accuracy. This technique is particularly useful for resource-constrained environments where computational resources are limited.

By implementing LoRA in AI model development, developers can create smaller and more efficient models that are well-suited for edge computing applications.

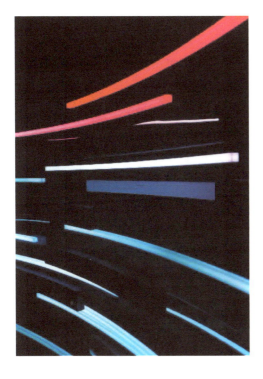

Quantization is another key technique for developing smaller AI models. By reducing the precision of the model's parameters, quantization can significantly decrease the memory footprint and computational requirements of the model. This approach is especially useful for applications where real-time processing is essential, such as in autonomous vehicles or IoT devices. By incorporating quantization methods into AI model development, developers can create leaner models that are both cost-effective and efficient.

Cost-effective optimization strategies are essential for democratizing AI technology. By leveraging techniques such as LoRA and quantization, developers can fine-tune AI models in a way that minimizes costs while maximizing performance. These strategies are particularly important for industries that are looking to adopt AI technology but may be constrained by budget limitations. By optimizing AI models in a cost-effective manner, businesses can unlock the full potential of AI technology and drive innovation in their respective fields.

In conclusion, the future of AI model development lies in creating smaller, more efficient models that can be deployed in a wide range of applications. Techniques such as Low Rank Adaptation (LoRA) and quantization are key to achieving this goal by reducing the computational complexity of AI models and optimizing their performance. By democratizing AI technology through smaller, more efficient models, developers can unlock new opportunities for innovation and drive progress in industries across the board.

Final Thoughts on Democratizing AI Technology

As we wrap up our discussion on democratizing AI technology, it is crucial to emphasize the importance of developing smaller, more efficient models. Techniques such as Low Rank Adaptation (LoRA) and quantization are revolutionizing the way we approach AI model development, making it more accessible and cost-effective for a wider range of users. By fine-tuning AI models using these methods, we can create high-performing models that are optimized for resource-constrained environments.

Democratizing AI: A Comprehensive Guide to Developing Smaller, More Efficient Models

Low Rank Adaptation (LoRA) techniques have proven to be highly effective in optimizing AI models, enabling developers to achieve better performance with reduced computational complexity. This approach allows for more efficient utilization of resources, making it possible to deploy AI models in edge computing applications where computational power is limited. By implementing LoRA in AI model development, we can maximize efficiency and reduce costs, ultimately democratizing AI technology for a broader audience.

Quantization methods also play a crucial role in developing smaller AI models that are more streamlined and efficient. By reducing the precision of numerical values in the model, quantization allows for significant reductions in model size without sacrificing performance. This technique is particularly useful for industries and applications where memory and processing power are limited, enabling the deployment of AI models in a wider range of settings.

Cost-effective optimization strategies are key to democratizing AI technology and making it more accessible to a broader audience. By leveraging techniques such as LoRA and quantization, developers can achieve significant improvements in model performance without the need for expensive hardware or extensive computational resources. This shift towards more efficient and cost-effective AI model development is opening up new possibilities for industries and applications that were previously out of reach.

In conclusion, the development of smaller, more efficient AI models is a game-changer for democratizing AI technology. By implementing techniques such as Low Rank Adaptation (LoRA) and quantization, developers can fine-tune models more effectively and cost-efficiently, making AI technology more accessible to a wider range of users. These advancements in AI model optimization are paving the way for a future where AI technology is more inclusive and impactful across industries and applications.

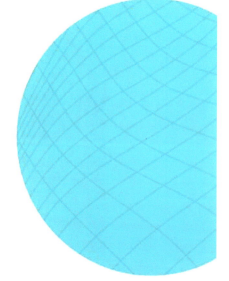